What is the difference between Girls and Boys?

Boys Edition

written by
Alicia Prescott

Copyright © 2017 Alicia Prescott
All rights reserved.
ISBN-13: 978-1542946513
Printed by CreateSpace, An Amazon.com Company

This book is dedicated to
my sweet kitty-boy, Max.

To my wonderful, supportive husband, Matt,
and our cosmic course correction, Evelyn.
...a very special THANK YOU!!

This book aims to help kids learn about how their bodies function, encourage personal body autonomy, and normalize healthy self exploration.

Some parents may find the content too graphic for their child's maturity level.

What is the difference between Girls and Boys?

I'll give you a hint: it's NOT about

It's about their bodies:
the place in between

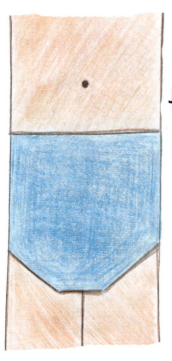

the bottom of their waists

and

the tops of their knees.

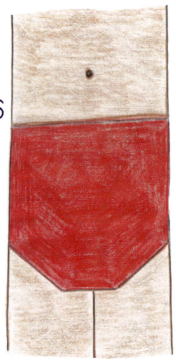

and we'll talk about girls some other day.

It's all about

BOYS

and their bodies today!

Some boys are BIG,

some boys are small ~

Penises, too, come in different shapes and sizes...

(intact/uncircumcised)

(circumcised)

And sometimes penises seem full of surprises...

 like how they can **Dance,**

and how they can **Wiggle;**

how they move on their own ~  it makes me **Giggle!**

They can magically stiffen ~ and point in the
upward direction.

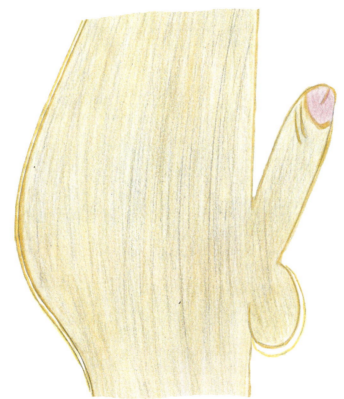

It's totally normal.
It's called an **erection.**

Lots of things cause it. Mostly stuff that you like.

Erections even happen in the middle of the night.

If you want it to soften, back to how it once was,

then think something new like:

just **how** do bees buzzzzzzzz?

Some call it a "BONER",

but bones, there are not...

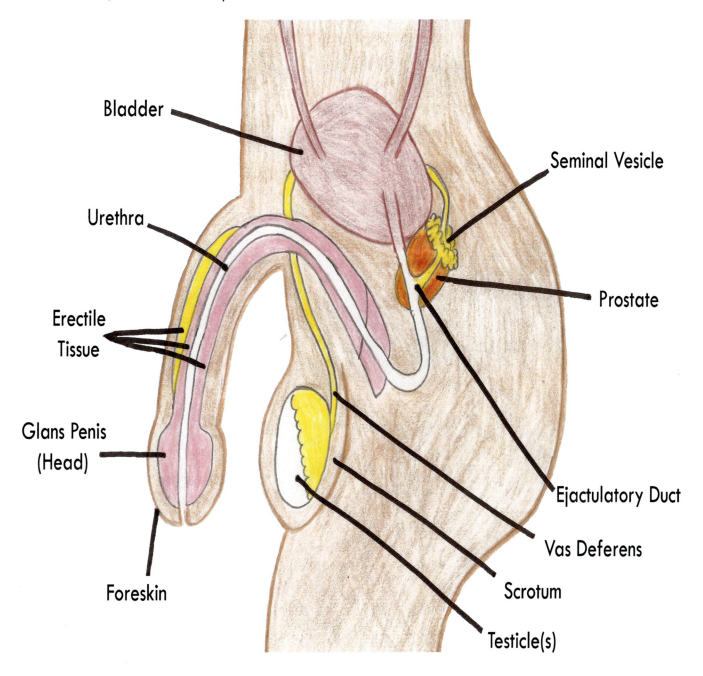

Your penis hangs around
with his two closest buds;

you can call them

your balls,

royal jewels,

or just nuts.

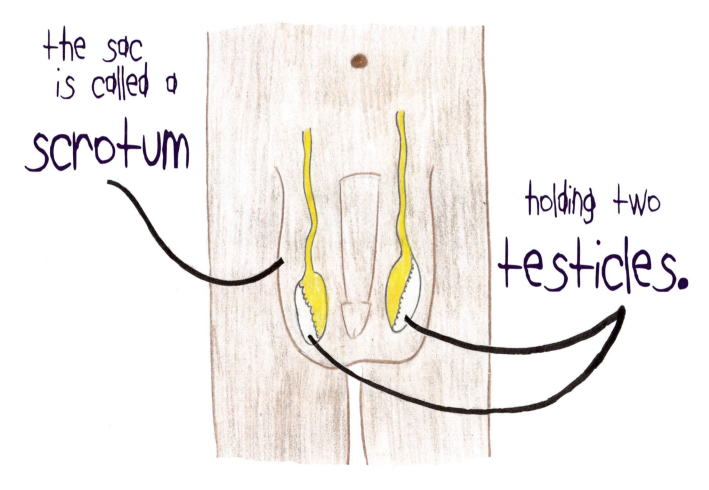

When you play that way,
it's called:

ma-stur-bate.

When they swim their way to a girl's private parts,

then a BABY can form, who will warm all our hearts.

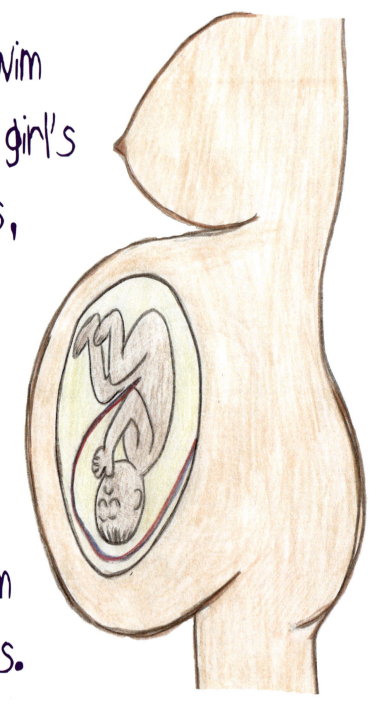

But you're not ready yet, mind, body, or brain;

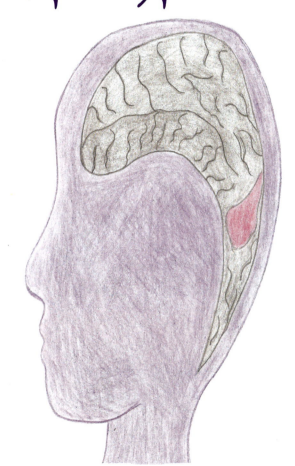

many things must first happen and your body must change.

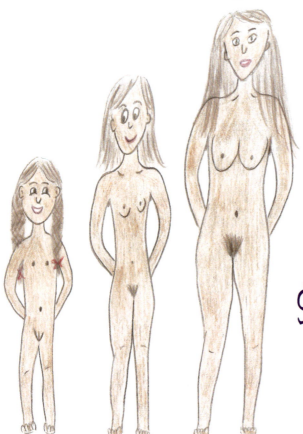
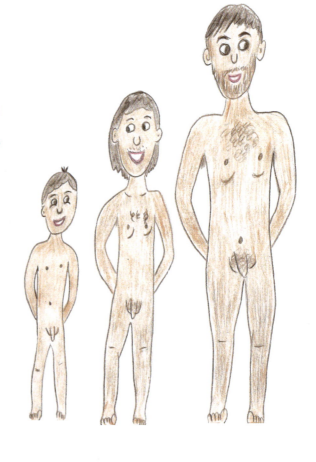

Your body will change as you grow a bit more.

You'll find hair in new places; new things to explore!

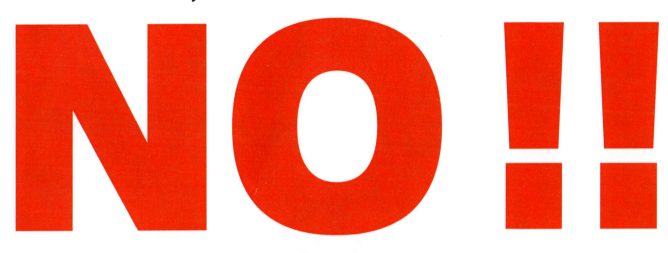

But <u>no matter what</u> others think, do, or say,

just follow your heart and you'll be okay.

So for now, find a comfortable place of your own

where you can sit and play with your bone.

Made in United States
North Haven, CT
11 June 2023

37630814R00022